# MOUNT EVEREST

*by Nadia Higgins*

a Capstone company — publishers for children

*Engage Literacy* is published in the UK by Raintree.
Raintree is an imprint of Capstone Global Library Limited, a company incorporated in England and Wales having its registered office at 264 Banbury Road, Oxford, OX2 7DY – Registered company number: 6695582

www.raintree.co.uk

Editorial credits
Erika L. Shores, editor; Richard Parker, designer; Wanda Winch, media researcher; Katy LaVigne, production specialist

Image credits
Alamy Stock Photo: Christian Kober 1, 32-33, Danita Delimont, 21, imageBROKER, 7, robertharding, 25; AP Images, 49; Getty Images Inc: AFP/Courtesy of Pemba Dorje Sherpa, 41, 55, AFP/Namgyal Sherpa, 59, 61, Ben Pipe Photography, 19, Christian Kober, 30; iStockphoto: fotoVoyager, 17, isoft, 52-53; Minden Pictures: Doug Allan, 28-29; National Geographic Creative: Barry Bishop, 51, 57, Cory Richards, 23; Newscom: robertharding/Christian Kober, 35, Zuma Press/Bogati/Nawang Sherpa, 36, Zuma Press/Outside/Michael Brown, 42-43, Zuma Press/Serac Adventure Films, 38; Shutterstock: Cube29, 27, Daniel Prudek, 18, Galyna Andrushko, cover, Nick Fox, 15, Olga Danylenko, background image, Travfi, back cover, 5 (middle), Vadim Petrakov, 16, Vixit, 1, 27 (back), 62, wavebreakmedia, 13; SuperStock: imageBROKER, 9, 45, John Warburton Lee/John Warburton Lee, 10; Thinkstock: iStockphoto/DanielPrudek, 47

21 20 19 18 17
10 9 8 7 6 5 4 3 2 1
Printed and bound in China.

*Mount Everest*

ISBN: 978 1 4747 4592 5

# CONTENTS

# THE ROOFTOP OF THE WORLD

No place on Earth is higher than Mount Everest. Its *summit*, or highest point, is often called the Rooftop of the World. The mountain's snowy peak is a record-breaking 8,850 metres in the air.

Other snow-capped peaks surround Mount Everest in all directions. Their jagged tops poke up through the clouds. Everest peers above the other peaks in the Himalayan Mountain range on the continent of Asia.

Two countries lay claim to Everest. Tibet, an ancient country that is now part of China, is on the north side. Tibetans call the mountain *Chomolungma*, which means Goddess Mother of the World. On the southern side is Nepal. To the Sherpa people of this country, the mountain is *Sagarmatha*, or Forehead in the Sky.

**FACT**

The Himalayas are still growing. The landmasses on which the mountain range sits are still shifting. They rise by about 5 centimetres every year.

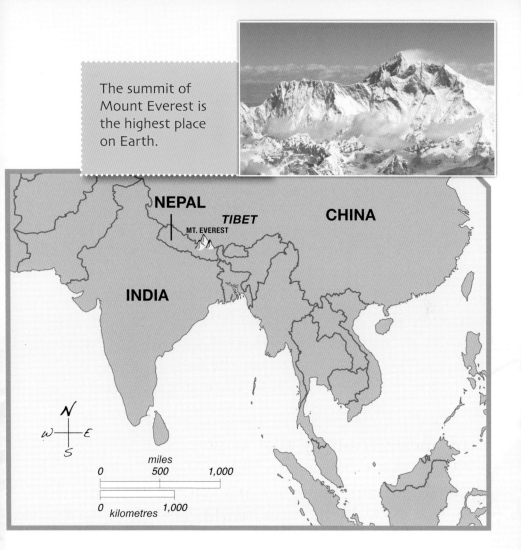

The summit of Mount Everest is the highest place on Earth.

NEPAL

TIBET

MT. EVEREST

CHINA

INDIA

N
W—E
S

miles
0     500     1,000

0   kilometres   1,000

How did the Himalaya range form and give rise to Earth's highest peak? It all began 60 million years ago when one landmass crashed into another. This pushed the sea floor separating the two giant pieces of land upwards to form a series of ridges, or folds. These folds of land are the towering Himalaya range.

What is it like on the Rooftop of the World? Some climbers say they can see Earth's round shape from Everest's summit. Earth's horizon bends at the edges. Looking down, climbers catch their breath as the ground appears to drop off in three directions.

At this *altitude*, the air is so thin, it holds about one-third of the oxygen that air holds at sea level. If a person landed at the summit suddenly, the lack of oxygen in the air would result in death after only a few minutes. But Everest climbers get their bodies ready for this challenge. They stretch out the climb for weeks by climbing short distances every day. Then climbers return to lower altitudes to breathe thicker air before heading back up the mountain again. By planning their climb in this way, their bodies can slowly adjust. Almost all climbers wear oxygen masks on the summit as well.

It is so cold at the summit, the thin air bites the skin. Even in May, temperatures dip well below zero. It is between minus 32 degrees and minus 26 degrees centigrade.

Climbers on Everest's summit look down at clouds covering jagged peaks.

Since 1953 roughly 4,000 climbers have made it to Everest's summit. For these climbers, this amazing act results in many emotions. For some, making it to the summit has been a lifelong dream. These climbers take grinning pictures. Using mobile phones, they call their loved ones to share the thrill. For others, reaching the summit is more serious. Between the vast sky and the steep cliffs, some climbers say they feel a great sense of smallness. They are tiny dots standing on the top of the world.

Climbers pose for a picture to celebrate their arrival on Everest's summit.

Sherpa guides are
paid to take climbers
to the summit.

At the opposite extreme are the many climbers who have only just made it to the top. Their legs are shaking from the demands of the climb. An Everest climber burns about 10,000 calories every day from exercise – five times the normal amount. Many lose a great deal of weight during the climb. The lack of oxygen is hard on their bodies as well. They are panting for breath. Their vision is blurred, and their minds may feel confused.

Unlike these other groups, Sherpa climbers have often been to the top at least once. Sherpas make their living by guiding tourists up the mountain. They see each climb to the summit as a gift from a goddess whose spirit they believe rests in the peak. During each successful summit, they put their hands together in thanks.

More than any other group, the Sherpas understand the changing whims of this mountain. The journey back down weighs on their minds. This journey is even more dangerous than the ascent. Sherpas pray for *tsin-lap* for themselves and others. All the climbers will need their sharpest wits for a safe journey back to camp.

# CLIMB TO THE TOP

Climbing to the summit of Mount Everest is too extreme for many people to ever consider. First of all, it costs a lot of money. Combining travel expenses, equipment, guides and climbing *permits*, a trip up Everest can cost between £30,000 and £80,000. Climbers need to have written permission, or a permit, before climbing. Most climbers also have to take two whole months off of work. They undergo months of physical training to prepare for the fitness test of a lifetime.

Climbing Everest is also dangerous. *Avalanches*, falls, extreme cold and *hypoxia* (lack of oxygen) kill climbers almost every year. In 2016 alone, six people died on the mountain. It is said about five people die for every 100 who reach the summit. Also, a climber should not expect to even reach the top. About half the climbers end up turning back. This is due to altitude sickness, the extreme physical demands or bad weather on the mountain.

Climbing on an indoor climbing wall is just one way people prepare to climb Everest.

Despite the risks, every year more people attempt to climb Everest than the previous year. Why are climbers willing to risk so much? The challenge excites them. They seek the thrill of the adventure. Many want to test the limit of their own physical strength. They want to climb Everest to see if they can do it.

## The journey begins

People who choose to climb Everest can climb it in different ways, but one route is by far the most common. Climbers fly to Kathmandu, the capital of Nepal, in late March. That gives them enough time to reach the summit in early to mid-May. Timing a climb is key. Most of the year, the *jet stream*, a strong current of air, roars across the top of the mountain. In May, however, the jet stream skirts north of the mountain, causing the hurricane-like winds to die down.

**FACT**

In 2016 more than 400 people tried to reach the top of Everest. They included 288 climbers from around the world and more than 100 Sherpas and guides.

The city of Kathmandu is home to almost 1 million people.

From Kathmandu, climbers board small planes and fly to the mountain village of Lukla, Nepal. At 2,880 metres, many climbers are already feeling the effects of the thin air. They suffer from headaches and coughs as their bodies adjust.

In Lukla the climbers meet their Sherpa guides. These local people set up the trails their clients will follow. Sherpas also set up the camps in advance. They offer advice, medical aid and perform rescues, often at great personal risk.

A group of workers, called porters, carry the climbers' equipment from Lukla to Everest's *Base Camp*, the main camp on Everest. Porters come from all over Nepal. The dangerous and difficult work of being a porter pays better than many other jobs in Nepal.

Yaks bring climbing supplies to Base Camp.

Porters are employed to haul huge loads of supplies for climbing teams.

A single porter can carry a load of 30 kilograms or more. A porter carries a load on his or her back, balancing it with a strap around the forehead. More equipment is piled onto brown shaggy yaks. These long-haired animals form a line along the path. Their collar bells clank as they move along.

Climbers spend about a week walking through the Khumbu Valley to Base Camp. The forests here are lush and green. Climbers walk among pine trees and plants with huge flowers. They follow streams that wind through hills of barley crops.

Rhododendrons are one of the plants climbers see on the trek to Base Camp.

Musk deer live as high up as 5,000 metres in the Himalayas.

Along the way, they rest at Sherpa villages. Climbers get to taste local food, such as potato pancakes with yak butter. A climber may put on a white silk scarf, called a kata. Sherpas believe this scarf offers protection for the journey.

# Base Camp

As climbers approach Base Camp, the air gets even colder. The landscape starts to change. Few trees grow here. Rocks and snow line the path to Base Camp.

Base Camp lies at the bottom of a *glacier*, a slow-moving river of ice. The Khumbu Glacier starts high up on Everest. It ends here, at 5,334 metres.

At Base Camp, many small tents sit on an ice field covered with rocks. Colourful flags hang above the tents, flapping in the wind. The busy camp provides many comforts, such as internet access and showers. Doctors are here, too. A helicopter landing pad lies ready for emergency rescues.

## Doctors at Everest

In 2003 Dr Luanne Freer started a clinic at Base Camp. The doctors here are trained in treating illnesses caused by climbing and high altitude. They work in a medical tent during the Everest climbing season.

Small tents sit on the cold, rocky ground at Base Camp.

Climbers will spend many weeks at Base Camp. They take short trips up the mountain. Then they come back down to sleep. These trial runs help their bodies adjust to the air. However, lack of oxygen causes sleepless nights for many people. Climbers battle severe headaches and hacking coughs. Diarrhoea is also common, the result of drinking melted snow that is dirty.

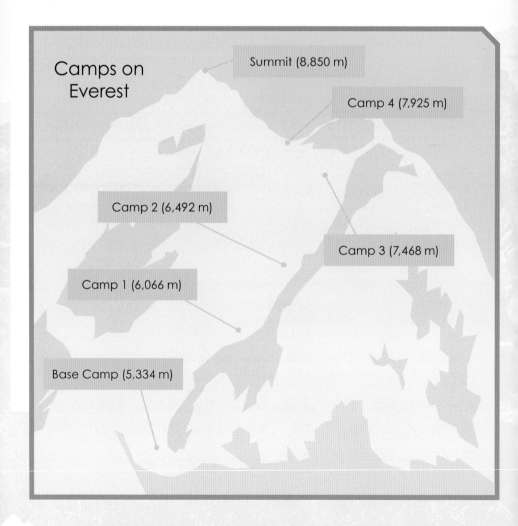

Camps on Everest

Summit (8,850 m)

Camp 4 (7,925 m)

Camp 2 (6,492 m)

Camp 3 (7,468 m)

Camp 1 (6,066 m)

Base Camp (5,334 m)

Before they leave for the summit, a climbing team holds a special ceremony.

When the time comes for a climbing *expedition* to push to the summit, Sherpas and climbers perform a special ceremony called a puja. They burn juniper branches. They believe the sharp-smelling smoke brings blessings upon them. The climb to the top of Everest begins soon after.

# The Khumbu Icefall

The first part of the climb from Base Camp is the most difficult. The Khumbu Icefall forms as the Khumbu Glacier tumbles over a drop-off. A normal river would form a waterfall. But this frozen river turns into towering walls of ice called *seracs*. A single serac can be as high as a six-storey building. Between the ice blocks, *crevasses*, or cracks, plunge down as far as 30 metres.

The icefall is always shifting. It shifts a metre or so down the mountain every day. A serac may collapse or a crevasse may rip open at a moment's notice.

For the Sherpa climbers, the icefall is especially dangerous because they spend more time there than anyone else. These local guides find the best route through the icefall every year. They set out ahead of their clients and set up ropes, placing them into the ice with special ice screws or pickets. They tie metal ladders across the crevasses to make bridges.

Climbers must cross giant cracks in the ice using ladders that have been roped together.

Once the route is set, a skilled climber can scale the icefall in just a few hours. A climber uses clips called *carabiners* to attach to the ropes. These ropes connect to the climber's harness, which he or she wears around the waist and thighs. If a climber slips, the ropes should stop the fall. On their shoes, climbers wear metal claws called *crampons*. These claws dig into the ice and make it easier to climb.

The ice creaks and pops as it shifts and melts. Climbers often hear the sounds of a crashing serac. It sends their hearts racing. But they must quickly turn back to the task at hand. Paying close attention, they take their next careful step.

# Everest gear

oxygen mask

carabiners

backpack

ice pick

ascenders

harness

ropes

crampons

boots

## The Valley of Silence

Climbers reach Camp 1 at the top of the Khumbu Icefall. This camp is about 2,740 metres from the summit. It is best for a climber to rest for one night at this small camp. In the morning, he or she heads out for a new challenge – the Valley of Silence. This peaceful valley is also known as the Western Cwm (pronounced KOOM).

After reaching the top of the Khumbu Icefall, climbers arrive at the Valley of Silence.

The Valley of Silence is a box canyon. Around this wide, flat area are nearly vertical walls of snow and ice. The sun reflects off the snow on the ground as well as the sides. This makes temperatures rise quickly. As the sun comes up into the sky, it can go from below zero to 32 degrees centigrade. As the journey wears on, climbers peel off layer after layer of clothing. They try to cool off with handfuls of snow, but the snow instantly melts against their hot skin.

The sun is very bright. Climbers wear hats and dark goggles to protect their eyes. Sun this bright could make them go blind for hours or even days. They coat their skin with sunscreen and rub thick balm on their lips.

Even though the climb here is fairly gentle, the altitude is still going up and the air keeps getting thinner. Between the heat and the lack of oxygen, climbers become exhausted. Taking off a jacket or lifting a bottle can take a lot of effort.

Guides watch for signs of dangerous heat stroke among their clients. These signs include feeling sick, being confused and painful muscle cramps. They know that even on the snowy slopes of Everest, heat can be a killer.

The sun's rays reflect off the white snow in the Valley of Silence.

# The Lhotse Face

Finally, at 6,492 metres climbers arrive at Camp 2. They are now roughly 2,400 metres from the summit. Their trek from Camp 1 to Camp 2 takes about nine hours. This roomy camp has more comforts than the last one. A hot meal and a chance to wash up await.

After a rest, climbers brace themselves for the next leg of the trip. They put on their warmest gear. They begin the hard climb up the Lhotse Face. This icy blue surface is the western side of the nearby Lhotse Mountain.

At Camp 2 climbers put on their warmest clothes and prepare for the next part of their journey.

## Bathroom breaks

Climbers must follow special rules about going to the bathroom on Everest. Liquid goes in bottles, which they empty only at certain spots. Other waste gets packed into bags and cans and then carried down the mountain. These rules must be carefully followed because climbers drink melted snow. If human waste gets into snow, it can cause disease.

For this slippery climb, climbers clip onto ropes that have been attached to the mountain by Sherpas. Metal objects called *ascenders* slide up and down, then lock in place. They give the climbers something to grip as they slowly make their way up the mountain.

This part of the route can be very slow. This high up, the air is so thin that the body can no longer adjust. Climbers gasp for air, and they pause on the ropes to rest. They simply do not have the energy to move quickly.

At the height of climbing season in May, the ropes can be so crowded that it's dangerous. A climber may have to wait in a queue for hours to take their turn. Sitting still in below-zero temperatures can numb climbers' fingers, toes and faces. Even when protected by the warmest gear, frostbite can occur. Everest climbers have lost fingers and toes due to frostbite.

Climbers hold onto a rope as they slowly make their way upwards.

Camp 3 is in constant danger of avalanches.

Climbers also watch each other for signs of a deadly drop in body temperature, called *hypothermia*. These signs include being confused and sleepy. If this happens, the climber will need medical care straight away to warm up his or her body.

Halfway up the Lhotse Face, climbers stop at Camp 3. This is about a six-hour climb from Camp 2. This small camp sits on a ledge carved into the side of the mountain. Climbers strap their tents down to this icy perch. They wiggle into their narrow sleeping bags and try to sleep. They gather their strength for a difficult day of rock climbing ahead of them.

In the morning, they clip back onto the ropes, and the crawl up the Lhotse Face begins again. At the top, the ice gives way to rock. Climbers go up a limestone cliff called the Yellow Band. After that, they face one last hurdle before the next camp. They climb up a snow-covered wall of rock called the Geneva Spur.

# The Death Zone

The final part of the Everest climb is sometimes called the Death Zone. It is the place where nothing can survive for long. The Death Zone starts at about 7,900 metres. It is about 900 metres from the top of Everest. This high up, very few people can continue without the help of oxygen masks. A severe lack of oxygen can lead to deadly brain swelling. It can cause fluid build-up in the lungs that can make a person feel like he or she is drowning.

Camp 4 is in the area called the South Col.

Maybe even more dangerous than this, reduced oxygen can cause poor judgment. A person may not be able to make good decisions about their safety. They may not decide if and when to turn back due to bad weather or altitude sickness. An oxygen mask is not a magic solution. It makes up for only about 900 metres of altitude. Even with a mask, 7,900 metres still feels like 7,000 metres.

Camp 4 sits at the base of the Death Zone on an area called the South Col. The wind roars over this rocky field so quickly and loudly that it can drown out voices. Whipping winds rattle the tents. Guides keep a close eye on the sky as blizzards can blow in quickly and cause whiteouts. The blowing snow makes it impossible to see more than a metre or so ahead.

## Bodies on Everest

Climbing the South Col, climbers may be startled by a terrifying sight. Some 280 people have died climbing Everest, and some of their bodies remain where they fell. The frozen bodies are too heavy to remove this high up on the mountain. Climbers have no choice but to quietly walk past the remains of those who have gone before, their bodies preserved by the cold.

Climbers only stay a few hours at this camp to rest before their final climb to the top. At about 11pm they begin their summit push. From here, the rest of the trip is a race against the clock, as it takes 10 hours to reach the top. Climbers aim to arrive at the summit at about 9am. That will give them enough time to get back to the camp before dark. Climbing down in the dark is too dangerous. Many climbers have had to turn around just short of the summit because they have fallen behind schedule.

Climbers ascend the South Col by the light of their headlamps. They file along, one by one, along a fixed rope.

The final push to the summit begins in darkness.

After about five hours, climbers reach the Balcony, a flat, icy area where they stop and rest. By now, the sun is coming up. Climbers take in the beautiful sight of dawn on the Himalayas. The sky bathes the nearby peaks in orange light.

Next, climbers forge through waist-deep snow to the South Summit. This hump of snow is not the real summit. This resting spot lies just 100 metres from the top. Climbers take the opportunity to put in a fresh oxygen bottle. They will need the boost for the next part of their journey.

The sun rises as climbers near the summit of Everest.

# The climb to the top

Ahead of them lies the Cornice Traverse. They need to pay very close attention in order to climb this ice-capped ridge. Steep drops plunge down a metre from the path. Without the ropes, a fall would mean certain death. The pace becomes extremely slow on this narrow edge. Climbers make their way at about five seconds per step.

At last, climbers arrive at their final challenge – the Hillary Step. This spot can be backed up with traffic jams. People wait their turn to scale this 12-metre wall of rock and ice and reach the top of the mountain. After this, a short hike leads to their main goal – the Rooftop of the World. They celebrate with hugs and pictures, but they cannot stay long. The return journey awaits them.

Just who were the first people to brave climbing the mighty Everest? And who are the people who live in the shadows of the Rooftop of the World?

In this photo, climbers approach the Hillary Step.

# RECORD BREAKERS

For hundreds of years, the Sherpa people have built their villages at the base of Mount Everest. For most of that time, they lived off this extreme land. They cut fields into the sides of hills, like shelves. They grew barley and potatoes, and they reared yaks. Sherpas lived in villages as high as 4,260 metres. But they never thought of climbing the mountain themselves because it was a holy site to be respected from a distance.

That way of life began to change in the 1920s. By then Everest was widely known as the highest mountain in the world. Climbers from Great Britain arrived aiming to be the first people to reach the mountain's peak.

British explorers needed help from the Sherpas. The local people had lived so long in Everest's shadows that their bodies were adapted to the thin air.

Although they had not tried climbing Everest before, Sherpas found that they were naturally skilled at it. They took jobs carrying loads and finding new routes. This new work was exciting, and it paid well. The Sherpa way of life began to change.

Namche Bazaar is a Sherpa village located at 3,440 metres above sea level.

After the early climbs by the British, the dream of reaching Everest's peak went unmet. Starting in 1921, 15 expeditions had set out and failed. Twenty-four climbers died during these early attempts. Finally, on 29 May, 1953, Edmund Hillary of New Zealand and Sherpa Tenzing Norgay prepared for the final push to the top.

In the early morning darkness, they pulled on their leather boots and metal crampons. They strapped on their heavy oxygen equipment as well. By 9am, they reached the knife-edge of the Cornice Traverse. One of the men swung his axe to cut steps in the snow. They slowly made their way between the steep drops on either side. Next, they made their way to the final wall of rock and ice. Unlike climbers today, they had no ropes to hold onto. They wedged their bodies inside a crack and wriggled up to the top.

At 11.30am that morning, they took their final steps through deep snow. Hillary and Norgay became the first people to ever stand on the Rooftop of the World. They had found the route that most climbers still use today.

Edmund Hillary and Tenzing Norgay were the first climbers to reach the top of Everest.

## FACT

Hillary and Norgay's success was due in large part to the team of 350 porters, 20 Sherpas, eight other climbers and many tonnes of supplies.

Hillary shook Norgay's hand, and the Sherpa pulled him in for a hug and a slap on the back. Hillary took photos looking down all sides of the mountain to prove that he and Norgay had really made it to the top. Norgay said a prayer of thanks. He also buried some sweets in the snow as a gift to the goddess of the mountain. The two men spent just 15 minutes on the summit, but that was enough to make history.

Hillary and Norgay were Everest's first record breakers, but many more firsts were still to come. Everest offered new routes to try, new ways to climb. Who would be the first to climb up through its more difficult Western Ridge? In 1963 a US expedition took that prize. This team was made up of a group of scientists. They studied the mountain. They learned how the human body works under extreme stress with little oxygen.

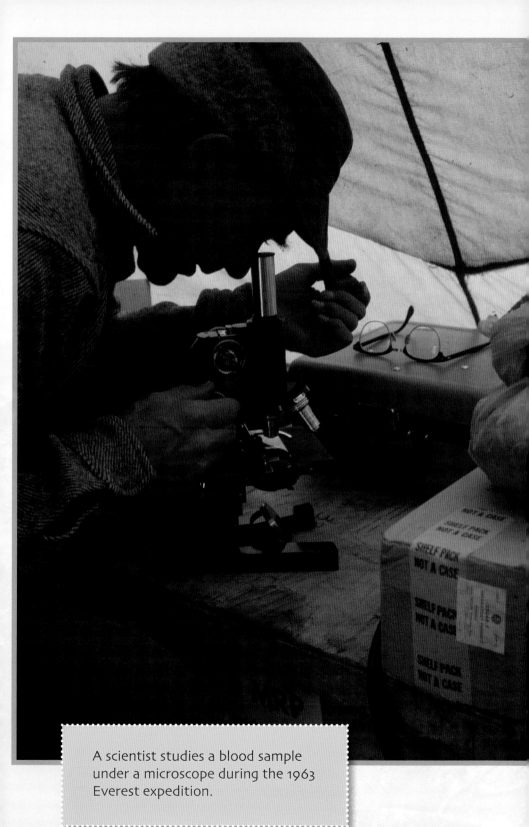

A scientist studies a blood sample under a microscope during the 1963 Everest expedition.

In 1975 the first woman reached the top. Junko Tabei from Japan climbed with an all-female expedition, helped by male Sherpas. Every year, climbers kept looking for new ways to outdo other record breakers.

In 1978 Reinhold Messner and Peter Habeler proved that a human could survive an Everest climb without the help of oxygen bottles. But Messner set his sights on an even more dangerous challenge. In 1980 he climbed again without oxygen. He also climbed by himself and without a radio to call for help. He became the first person to perform a solo climb up Everest.

In this photograph a paraglider is floating among the Himalayas.

In the 1980s, climbers kept finding new routes. In 1988 a French man sailed down from Everest's summit in a paraglider. Australian Tim Macartney-Snape was the first person to go from sea to summit. In 1990 he swam in the Bay of Bengal and then set out on a three-month trek to the Himalayas where he climbed Everest. In 2000 a man from Slovenia became the first to ever ski down from Everest's peak.

The following year, the first blind person, Erik Weihenmayer, reached the top. He is a climber from the United States. In 2004 the Sherpa guide Pemba Dorje scaled the entire mountain in just 8 hours and 10 minutes. That is the fastest time ever.

## MOUNT EVEREST RECORD BREAKERS

**1953**: Edmund Hillary and Tenzing Norgay, first to reach summit

**1975**: Junko Tabei, first woman to reach summit

**1978**: Reinhold Messner, first to reach summit alone and with no oxygen

**2001**: Erik Weihenmayer, first blind person to reach summit

**2004**: Pemba Dorje, fastest climb to the summit

**2010**: Jordan Romero, youngest person to reach summit

**2011**: Apa Sherpa, most times reaching the summit

**2013**: Yuichiro Miura, oldest person to reach summit

Jordan Romero of the United States became the youngest person to ever reach the summit. In 2010 he stepped onto the summit at the age of 13. Three years later, the oldest person, Yuichiro Miura from Japan, set the opposite record at the age of 80. Meanwhile, Sherpas keep climbing the mountain year after year. In 2011 Apa Sherpa stepped onto Everest's summit for the 21st time. No one on Earth has climbed to the Rooftop of the World more than he has.

Pemba Dorje

# PROBLEMS AND SOLUTIONS

Climbing Everest has changed a lot since the first summit in 1953. Back then, climbers wore itchy wool clothes and three pairs of gloves. Today, climbers have full-body suits made from quick-drying fabrics made to keep them warm and dry. In the 1950s, an oxygen system weighed about 11 kilograms compared with just 2 kilograms today. Modern climbers are also helped by GPS, weather reports, medical care and state-of-the-art rescue helicopters.

This picture from the 1963 US expedition that reached the summit shows the large masks and the backpacks holding oxygen equipment.

These changes have saved lives, but they have also caused some problems. They made it possible for climbing Everest to become a booming business. By the early 2000s, hundreds of climbers were flocking to Everest every season. Guide businesses led trips for those who could afford to pay the hefty fees. The mountain was not just for a few professional climbers anymore.

The crowds became a problem for the mountain. Everest's pure streams became polluted from human waste. The green forests at its base were thinning out. People were chopping down shrubs to burn as fuel at camp. Heaps of litter left behind by climbers were piling up on this sacred site.

Piles of rubbish are found on Everest at 8,000 metres.

Today, climbers are more careful about where they leave their waste. They use fuel instead of wood to cook at camp. Nepal's government has also taken action to regrow the tree cover at the mountain's base, though this will take many years.

In 2010 a group of Nepali climbers led a huge cleanup effort. They removed nearly two tonnes of litter near the Death Zone. Other cleanup teams have hauled down tents, cans, equipment and even human waste. The government of Nepal has also started charging climbers a £3,200 rubbish fee. Climbers agree to bring back a set amount of rubbish when they come back. If they fulfill their promise, they get their money back. If they do not, they lose their money. Many climbers now follow the principle of "leave no trace". They try not to leave a mark on the mountain.

In 2010 this group of climbers removed tonnes of rubbish left behind on Everest.

The Sherpa people have lived near it for centuries. Hundreds of climbers attempt to summit it every year. The towering Mount Everest has long captured the interest of people around the world. Its harsh, white frozen landscape is a powerful sight. When Edmund Hillary and Tenzing Norgay stepped foot on the summit of Everest, they proved that even the world's tallest peak could be conquered. Today the people of Nepal, Tibet, and those who come to climb it know this mighty giant is a place to protect and respect.

The summit of Everest is always covered in ice and snow.

# GLOSSARY

*altitude*   height of land, as compared to the level of the sea

*ascender*   object used in climbing that can be clipped to a rope to act as a foothold or handhold

*avalanche*   large mass of snow and ice that suddenly crashes down a mountain

*Base Camp*   main camp on Everest

*carabiner*   oval-shaped metal clip; climbers use carabiners to secure rope to ice anchors

*crampon*   metal device that snaps onto the bottom of a climber's boot; a crampon has sharp points for digging into ice

*crevasse*   deep crack in a glacier

*expedition*   group of people on a journey with a goal, such as climbing to a mountaintop

*glacier*   slow-moving river of ice

*hypothermia*   condition in which a person's body temperature becomes dangerously low

*hypoxia*   condition in which a person's body is not receiving enough oxygen

*jet stream*   strong wind at high altitudes that usually blows from west to east

*permit*   written statement giving permission for something

*serac*   towering block of ice on a glacier

*summit*   very top of a mountain

# INDEX